silent
scream

silent scream

j.m. morgan

for her

i've been
silent,
muffling
my *scream*,
for
so long,
be
gentle
with me.

contents

Preface

Every word that's written,
Fills me with fear,
Fear often displayed,
Of not belonging here.

The wretched language,
Written within each line,
Outlined on each stroke,
Streams through my mind.

Whines of trauma,
Rhymes of comfort,
Stanzas of pain,
Unveil my discomfort.

Shitty stanzas,
Horrible puns,
Capture life,
A battle not won.

End this,
I must,
But I know,
That she'll make a fuss.

I've closed this page several times,
Rewritten these verses aplenty,
Tried to put a bow on some of this shit,
That I've been dealing with.

This ain't pretty,
Nor is it raw,
Captured between these lines,
Is darkness' sole star.

These lines strung up,
Reveal my scars,
Although some healed,
Under these painful marks.

The telling of one's story,
Whether painful or empowering,
Is a valid part,
Of becoming whole.

Trigger and content warnings,
For the faint of heart,
Discomfort is valid,
In the name of art.

Wet eyes,
Break my disguise,
My demon's lies,
That I can't escape.

In each stanza,
Lies my blood,
Drained from my trauma,
Replenished by their karma.

Not part of some model,
Nor free,
My battle rages on,
This is me...

why write

words revealing the pieces of myself,
stringing together every statement,
mapping my every move.

why write?

writing is my therapy,
my confessional,
my sanctuary.

language manifests through my veins,
like tears flooding my face,
as my hand grapples the pen,
and sign my name underneath each tear.

writing tears,
tears writing themselves,
persevering through tears,
all takes strength, resiliency, and patience.

qualities I never knew I had...

the letter

dear teenaged me,
to the girl weeping in front of the toilet,
the girl whose tears flood the linoleum floor,
and stain the walls with her sorrow.

i'm sorry that you felt unloved,
unwanted,
in her home,
the home that we escaped to.

your tears should be of joy,
of laughter,
of majesty,
of future's wishes.

instead, your heart bares all,
like a transparent film,
like an open book,
like a pierced blade.

why must you linger so,
among the dingy floors of the bathroom,
in a pool of your own tears,
drowning within your own body.

don't you know the world is out there,
waiting on your performance,
requiring your presence,
and praying for your safe release.

the strikes,
the psychological scars of that voice,
those weapons,
those threats,
can't hurt you on this linoleum floor.

that trauma,
that pain,
that misery,
won't follow you towards that place.

breathe in,
breathe out,
soothe your whimpers,
silence your pain,
before another lash strikes your back.

dear teenaged me,
i wish i could tell you that shit gets better,
that your suffering wasn't in vain,
that your daily bathroom floods will cease.

the truth is,
i never got shit together,
never breathed,
never meditated,
never triumphed.

i always fought back,
and kept being met with resistance,
resistance in the form of violence,
violence disguised as the only means of controlling my
insanity.

no one doesn't seem to care,
not even the woman in the white coat,
who seems to read rehearsed lines,
and use tactics built for another struggle.

we can't go yet,
i've learned this truth,
for death by self solves nothing,
nor challenges our inner demons.

we must forget, hide, conceal,
wear our content mark for others,
lest we be ridiculed, shamed, and threatened.

dear teenaged me,
on the linoleum floor,
get off that cold dingy floor,
and wipe the dirt from your body.

keep your feet planted on the ground,
clear your eyes of your sadness,
hatred, and hopelessness,
steady your breath,
inhale, exhale.

now turn that doorknob,
and walk on the thin line,
between your existence,
and your truth.

darkness

Normal

It gets old after a while,
Using my emotions to write,
Mustering up enough strength,
To convey my thoughts on paper.

I've always written down my thoughts,
Words I dare not speak,
And force myself not to ever validate,
The things that go unspoken.

I never wrote twice about one singular experience,
Captured my life on paper like this,
Reopened old scars,
That I assumed healed under my scabs.

I don't know,
Never assumed anything was wrong,
Everyone has a personality,
and I figured the Lord ran out of time to create mine.

I remember one lady from my youth,
Asking why I look so solemn,
As if she understood,
The pains that I have experienced.

I remember one lady,
Asking me if I was alright,
Upon realizing that my face,
Appeared unhappy.

I remember the laughter,
So very clearly from my family,
Who was upset,
That I caused so much attention.

You see, I've always tried to blend in,
Tried to hide my face,
Attempted to force a smile,
To not ruin someone else's day.

I've become good at faking it,
Faking like I give a shit,
Feigning happiness,
All to not draw attention.

You see, we exist,
Although not visible to the naked eye,
Our spirits and souls are there,
If you just acknowledge difference.

I've always concealed my "difference" as indifference,
Indifference to life's outcomes,
Indifference to people,
And the alleged blessing of life.

Am I even human,
Can I feign happiness this long,
Not asking for help,
And not questioning if other people can see. Me.

Half of me is here,
Half of me is up there,
Part of me is down here,
While the other part is hidden elsewhere.

I can't fit that image,
Of that carefree girl,
Can't be saved,
From a world that never gave me a chance.

From the words of those women from my youth,
There's so much to be happy about,
So much to do,
And so much to expect.

Maybe if I pretended to care,
I wouldn't get all of this attention,
Pretended to make myself vulnerable,
And pull myself back in the nick of time.

Or maybe I should just write,
Write about these things,
Instead of talking about these things out loud,
To prevent myself from becoming these things.

I'll retreat to my safe place,
My eternal bathroom,
Where I first poured out my emotions,
To escape from here.

Sparks

I walked by,
the burning house to,
gaze inside the,
foggy windows.

The blazing fire cajoled,
me inside,
licked my neck,
ever so sweetly.

Gauging my soul,
To fulfill my dream of,
Searching for an answer to,
Heal my pain.

It comforted me with,
its arms it,
Stroked my back to,
Embrace me in its warmth.

A diamond ring emerged in,
The ring of fires to,
Propose to me and,
Be free.

I grabbed the ring and,
Put my body against the,
Fire to get,
what I yearned for.

Take Me

Fire,
Caressing me,
Light the match.

Take me first,
Burn me,
Into those divine ashes.

Watch my skin,
Drift away,
In ecstasy.

Forever Bleeding

Can you hear her whimpers,
Those silent thumps of pain and despair,
That precious red liquor,
Spurring from her veins.

That gash,
That scar,
That beautiful slit in the Earth,
Soothing the echoes,
Of her silent rebirth.

Her rotting flesh,
Decomposing on the Earth's soil,
The smell of despair in the air,
Fills her heavy heart.

So warm, so delicate, so damp,
Is that precious golden stream of relief,
Wrapped around each scar,
Caused by her inner turmoil.

The Earth drinks up that vibrant liquor,
Mistaking it for life's sole hydration,
The precious odor and aroma of her warmth,
Is devoured by the Earth's rays.

Soothing, captivating, relieving,
Among this landscape once called home,
Breathing easily among the corrupted air,
Filled with the sweet nectar of her soul.

Warmth, Serenity, Vanity,
The release of such mesmerizing fumes,
Enables a slow descent into a restful sleep,
A sleep so powerful,
So captivating,
So invigorating.

She rests now,
A rest like no other,
As her body wraps around the blade,
The blade of dreams,
The blade of life,
The blade of love.

Heartbeat stops,
Movement ceases,
As her warm skin melts into the Earth,
Slowly, cautiously.

Her gash,
Her scar,
Her beautiful slit on her skin,
Her soul can rest now,
Among her vibrant liquor on the Earth.

Pillow

I can't breathe with this across my face,
Smothering me,
Restricting me,
Choking me.

I can feel the hair in my nose struggling,
Struggling to find a clear passage,
Trying to find some oxygen,
To escape this compressed space.

The pillowcase starts to lose its firmness,
Oxygen starts to seep through the crevices,
I move my face closer,
To prevent my body's chance of escape.

Pressing,
Pushing,
Squeezing,
Believing.

Pushing,
Straining,
Draining,
Tense.

My heartbeat slows,
And steadies to a weakened thump,
My body starts gripping for air,
Gripping for life!

What is going on

I can't do it,
Never could,
Probably never will.

Escape

My sweet escape,
Happened here,
On the fabric covered couch,
Amongst my animal friends.

Tea parties,
Birthday parties,
Parties of celebration,
And happiness.

I can hear screaming,
in the background,
from in the kitchen,
and across the hall.

Huge footsteps,
Stump against the floor,
Screams of terror,
Cries of fright.

No,
I must ignore them,
And go back to,
The birthday party.

Yes,
Sweet little Stanley,
You're turning,
Eight today.

Little Rainbow,
Your little brother,
Is cheering,
You on.

Huge vibrations,
Of laughter,
Stream on,
The couch.

Loud sounds,
Of celebration,
With hate,
Coming through.

Dang it,
I can't concentrate,
On the party,
In my imagination.

Try harder,
To escape,
From this place,
Of pure anguish.

Stanley sits confused,
About my distraction,
From our,
Real world troubles.

I must try,
Harder to ignore,
The screams from,
The other room.

Concentrate,
Focus,
On the party,
In my fantasy.

Silence,
Creeps through,
From the room,
My prison.

The party resumes,
As everyone celebrates,
Stanley's birthday,
My happiness.

Room full of,
Friends crafted from,
My imaginary world,
My double life.

I want to,
Stay inside,
To be with,
My animal friends.

To live free,
To live inside,
My imagination,
My happy place.

To avoid reality,
The endless fighting,
To escape here,
To stay there.

Oh Stanley,
My best friend,
We'll soon be free,
Once we escape…

Voices

I can hear voices,
Thunder like voices,
From above my pillow,
Roaring from the other room.

Voices of aggression,
Heartache,
Annoyance,
And stupidity.

The house is hot again,
His blood boiling,
Her voice fearful,
Of his angry tone.

Erupting from the tan couch,
Thunder streams in,
His brows furrow,
At her innocence.

I can hear voices,
Tornado like voices,
In the other room,
From the beast.

Grunts of anger,
Cries of defeat,
Stomps of intimidation,
Tears of fear.

His need,
Of controlling the air,
The air that we feel,
That belongs to him.

I just wanna,
Fall back to sleep,
Without feeling,
The heat of his voice.

Clamping of dishes,
Fury of noise,
Voices like thunder,
Above my pillow.

My small body quivering,
At the thought of her voice,
Standing against his voice,
Resulting in no sleep.

I can't breathe,
From the fear,
That her cries,
Will flood my dreams.

I get up,
To resume my Bible reading,
As I do many times,
On these frightful nights.

Breathe slowly,
Hold in the tears,
Don't let them hear,
That you're awake.

The thunder dies down,
As he grows tired,
Of raising his voice,
And talking to her.

Though it's over,
He triumphs,
The hot house,
Prevails again.

Voices of aggression,
Seem to win,
In this house of cards,
At her expense.

Daddy's Arms

how would it feel,
to be wrapped,
inside daddy's arms,
to be held,
tightly,
between his towering mass,
to feel his sweat,
trickle down,
his face,
onto mine.

How would it feel,
to feel the warmth,
between two humans,
so closely knit,
as their skin bonds,
to be smothered,
deep between,
the flabs,
of strength,
as he soothes,
my heart's scars.

How would it feel,
for daddy's arms,
to not be distant,
to be here with me,
in this moment,
to stroke my arms,
to encapsulate his hand,
in mines,
to state his presence,
affirm his love,
for me,
us,
in spite of his abuse,
of our mother's gardens,
her presence,
her flaws,
weaved through,
mine.

how would it feel,
to not live,
in fear,
of days past,
of his voice,
resounding through,
the walls,
fear of presence,
from his roaring footsteps,
stomping on the floors,
fear of being afraid,
his shadow,
where nothing,
is there.

How would it feel,
to be,
daddy's little girl,
to see daddy's smile,
to hear him affirm,
his love for me,
to feel his,
rough hands,
around me,
hugging me,
her,
us,
five beings,
same love,
home,
wrapped inside,
daddy's arms.

Sunshine

Woke up,
To bright lights,
To sounds of packing,
To familiar faces.

Clothes cleared,
Rooms isolated,
Mother's tears,
And children's confusion.

Packed and loaded,
Into the silver SUV,
In the driveway,
To drive away.

From the home,
Our home,
From the forest,
And From my stage.

From my bee friends,
From the split tree,
My stage of happiness,
Alleviation from pain.

Of a second time,
Traveling,
Venturing,
Away from the *abuse*,

Emotional *abuse*,
From my father,
Pictures of her cries,
Amongst our toys.

His screaming,
At her flaws,
At his flaws,
From his aggression.

Arrival at our safe haven,
On her first try,
Of escaping from,
Her future self.

Her pathetic whimpering,
Of her *abuse*,
On a call,
With her *abuser*.

Failed promises,
Resort in her isolation,
Her final bid,
To regain her womanhood.

Keys jingle,
As her *abuser* travels,
Lights go on,
And tears flood.

Clothes packed once more,
Into garbage bags,
But this time,
Everything goes.

Sadness fills my heart,
That turns into anger,
As her *abuser* promised a vacation,
The last of many without her.

Loaded and packed,
Into her SUV,
Traveling abroad,
But a few towns over.

In another trailer,
On another large amount of land,
But surrounded by people,
And not by my imaginary world.

I hate this,
From sunshine to darkness,
From darkness to neutrality,
And from neutrality back to darkness.

Sunshine's lost victims,
The real victims,
Taken from their community,
And placed in another.

Sunshine,
From the abuser,
In spite of his accuser,
From the light of their children.

captured.

Rewind

Rewind
Reverse,
Undo,
This curse.

Release,
Relieve,
My arm,
My sleeve.

Dissipate,
Disperse,
Dissolve,
My spirit.

Destroy,
Demolish,
Dismantle,
My pain.

Erase,
Eliminate,
Expunge,
Her presence.

Birth

Ever thought about a life without a leech draining the
world's resources,
A life without my meaningless existence,
A world that is still able to sustain without my life.

This life is something that only I can imagine,
One that I reckon with,
A likeness that was created without interference from the
real world.

I struggle to breathe most days,
Struggle to sleep other days,
Struggle to find my resiliency all days.

Sometimes I dream about life not bore in that woman's
body,
A womb that I never voted for, longed for, nor prayed for,
To become a person that won't be doomed,
To be trapped in a public solitary confinement,
To face the snickers, the laughter, and the pointing from
some of Earth's precious gems.

Nowadays, my body has failed,
Only allowing me to get brief moments of sleep,
Allowing me to muster up enough energy,
To sustain myself for a few hours out of the day.

So yea,
I've thought about a life without her voice,
My absence,
My death,
And the warmth of dirt,
As it touches my deep skin,
And alleviates my pain.

A life without hearing her voice,
A voice so gut wrenching, so draining, so debilitating,
That makes me want to kill her, but mostly myself,
Just for the sake of escaping and maybe getting the sleep
I've dreamt of.

The kind of sleep that erases thoughts of her raising me,
Keeping me alive thus far,
As if I was destined to live with these scars,
Or to save her from hers.

This smile, this childish joy, and this patience,
Has always been a ruse,
To keep my identity shielded from outsiders,
To not let people blame me for my own emotions,
And not become the liquidator of such idiotic responses.

If I ever grow up,
I'll probably reflect back to that moment,
Every day like I usually do,
Back to that bathroom floor,
Sobbing my insanity away,
And rationalizing my emotions in a world that reminds me
of my privileges.

To the ones that I let down,
To the ones I hid from,
To the future little one that I won't have,
I extend my deepest apologies.

For living,
For breathing,
For wasting your time,
With my existence.

I often wonder if this is how others feel,
Living without meaning,
Living outside the borders of the world,
Existing in solitary.

Why, I ask,
What's my role,
My purpose,
And my story.

I must retreat to that border,
Along those crossroads,
Between this world and I,
To not disrupt the world's balance.

I can't leech on the world's resources any longer,
Nor exist in a bubble created solely for my demise.

I retreat to that safe haven,
To my own border,
Searching, dreaming, speculating,
Of a life without existence,
And a world that carries on without me.

Don't fret

Don't fret little child,
Dry your eyes.
It'll be ok,
Just you rise.

Inhale exhale,
Until you feel your heartbeat steady,
Look towards the sky,
When you're ready.

Ask those clouds,
To stop raining on your face,
Command that storm,
To make its haste.

Stop that weeping gal,
Before I strike your arm,
I told you before,
That God will keep you warm.

Don't tell me 'bout no pain,
When pain doesn't exist,
Those tears are full of deceit,
Now stand up to persist.

You're beautiful,
Without those tears,
You're more powerful,
Without those fears.

Don't fret my child,
Look towards the sky,
Watch the sky wipe you,
Like oceans running dry.

Be strong,
Be righteous,
You're valiant,
And priceless.

There's no strength in sorrow,
In those storms in your heart,
Nor that pain on your face,
That you use to drive us apart.

Fret not,
For your heavenly father has already healed you,
He'll accept your forgiveness,
And I will too.

There you go,
Rise to dry your eyes,
For help comes,
To those focused on the prize.

Inhale exhale,
Feel your heartbeat steady,
Now point your eyes towards the sky...
You're ready.

The Belt

The wrath of the brutality
Everlasting pain of its reign,
Heartache of the child,
Cries from each slash.

Love once demonstrated by rewards,
Turns into chastisement,
The wrath never loses course,
Following the delicate skin of the child.

Mobility arises from afar,
Child feels unloved and runs,
Through the forest and under the bridge,
Becomes a safe place for the time being.

Marks become a momentous reward,
The fact of disobedience stays in mind,
Breaths of silence follows,
The death from the belt.

Emotionless

Feeling powerless,
Powerless over the things,
That I can't alter.

Choking on my imperfections,
Struggling to express,
The discontent within.

Feeling incomplete,
Desolate,
Alone in a full room.

Reactions are mute,
Emotions are numb,
Voices screech.

Can't express,
For fear of rejection,
Their fear of my voice.

Penniless thoughts,
Pennies for my thoughts,
Dime sized Scars.

Release me from this chasm,
Remove your foot,
From upon my throat.

Struggling to find voice,
My voice,
From beneath this foot.

Mutters seep through,
Very faint,
So soft.

Another foot presses on my stomach,
A hand gags my mouth,
No sound.

Struggling to voice myself,
My voice,
From under this force.

Eyes of blood,
Words of terror,
Strangling me to remain silent.

Mute reactions,
Numbness,
Powerless in a world of people.

Not allowed to express,
Condemned with threats,
That I can't bear to confess.

Open close,
My mouth they did,
My tongue is removed,
Emotionless kid.

Mama Sees

Domino's,
Fat ho,
Mama's words,
Dirty curse.

Tight sleeves,
Can't breathe,
Mama sees,
My defeat.

Ignore,
Filthy words,
Stand tall,
Don't sulk.

The chin,
It sags,
Its fat,
Mama says.

Ignore,
Her insecurities,
Reflected onto,
My body.

Don't let her,
See my wet eyes,
Lest it might,
Stroke her ego.

She,
Rejects,
The body that,
I've produced.

Produced from,
Filthy words,
Merciless coping,
For the pain.

Why must,
She recap,
Me of the,
Body I inhabit.

I'm aware,
Of the way,
My body assembles,
Inside these sleeves.

Domino's,
Soothed,
The aches,
She wrought.

Her eyes,
Stare at me,
In disgust,
Of what she birthed.

I'm aware,
Of the flabs,
Of the sags,
Of the bulges.

I have,
The same eyes,
Bestowed from,
Your womb.

You won't,
Find a job,
With that body,
Mama says.

Her paranoia,
I succumb,
To her lies,
From her insecurities.

What's hers,
Is mine,
The insecurities,
The self-deprecation.

Push *it* back,
Tighten *it*,
Fix *it*,
Mama says.

Mama can't,
See the pain,
She inflicts,
From her tongue.

I just,
Want her,
To see that,
I see.

The flaws,
The flabs,
The sags,
The bags.

It's from,
The brain,
Wired to believe,
Her lies.

As evidenced,
Throughout years,
Of internalizing,
Her insecurities.

Not
Good
Enough.

Mama stop,
Pointing at *it*,
As if,
It will alter.

I think mama can,
See the pain,
She inflicts,
From her tongue.

I can't,
Live in fear,
Of what,
She may say next.

Fuck,
I gotta,
Get out,
Leave.

Mama sees,
Mama knows,
Mama makes me believe,
Mama makes me bleed.

Lurker

the dark haired, bronze eyed girl lingers now,
upon her journey,
from the broken home,
remembering the truth it once held.

stumbling against her soul,
fragments from her tears,
acknowledging the fact,
that nothing is actually there.

the footsteps that bear on her shoulder,
the chains beneath her knees,
straddle alongside her fragile body,
that once retained her life.

the sun blows a hurtful kiss,
at the lone girl on the narrow path,
her eyes weakened from temptation,
of withdrawing from the journey.

her hands form scars rougher than mountains,
the prairie she approaches fades to black,
the sparrows poke at her crumbled skin.

the tree provides support from her burden,
as she sits up on the ground,
to inquire a prayer,
and search for an easy escape.

all her life she longed for beauty,
and happiness,
but the lake will someday awaken her,
but her rosary will remain.

Unhand Me

Lips, so spiteful,
Consequences, so horrendous,
Life, so precious?
No, life so pointless.

Hands, so forceful,
Threats, so meaningless,
Pain, so painful?
No, pain so sweet.

The way,
Her pain,
Touched my veins,
The way,
My smile,
Illuminated from her child.

Voices, so loud,
Disappointment, so vile,
Strikes, so intense?
No, strikes so breathtaking.

The dishes,
In the sink,
Set her on the brink.
The lint,
On the floor,
Slapped her at the door.

Remove your hands,
From upon my arms,
That you inflicted undo harm,
Unhand me,
You wicked woman,
With this hate you summoned.

Her lover, so ruthless,
Gifted her,
Sticks, so painful?
No, sticks so spiteful.

My sweet cries,
Appeased the beast,
To say the least.
Her constant pleas,
For love nonexistent,
From my heart so resistant.

Lips, so pathetic,
Consequences, so pointless,
Love, so foreign,
No, love so heartless.

Time

Laid up,
Broken,
Shattered,
Desecrated.

Envisioning future's presence,
Memories,
Mementos,
Shadows.

Flashbacks now,
Of failure,
Of Anguish,
Of sad.

Could these scars be made whole,
Repaired,
Fixed,
Sealed.

Records avoid present,
Screeching,
Halting,
Repeating.

Time stables,
Time grabbles,
Pieces of me,
Time's pieces.

Drink Up

The tears fall from the eye,
Cloak my cheek and surround my mouth,
I drink up.

As I climb the mountain,
The weight gets heavier,
I grow short of breath.

I rest now,
But background voices strike my back,
And leave deep scars that can never heal.

Going back to the day I used to look up to her,
When I sat on the porch awaiting her return,
And caressing her in my arms.

Distant memories burn,
Cause of the mountain I must climb,
Will I ever reach it?

Her hateful words bring me to a ledge,
My tears make the ledge crumple,
But I catch onto a branch and keep going.

I grow thirsty,
Because of the tears I lost,
I descend now into my abyss.

The tears are moist,
They trail me behind,
But they can't make it.

I reach for my bottle,
And catch the tears,
I drink up.

The top looks more dismal than the bottom,
Full of many rivers that I have created,
The rivers that I filled with my tears.

She stands behind me now,
Striking my back,
My legs grow weak.

I look down at what I overcame,
I catch my tears in my hands,
I drink up.
I smile.

released?

It

Pill popping,
Skin cutting,
Body scarring,
Stomach growing.

The swallow,
The pain,
The marks,
The hunger.

Gulp,
Slit,
Scratch,
Digest.

Repeat.

Trauma,
My little piece of karma,
My reward,
My end.

Failure erupts,
Voices confirm,
The truth,
The fate.

Perceived failure caused this,
Self-punishment caused this,
Years caused this,
Unsureness resulted in…THIS.

Swallowing pills,
Breaking skin,
Creating bruises,
Eating…

Eating the pain,
The guilt,
The shame,
The unsureness… that's eating me!

Eating to stay calm,
To ignore the trauma,
To ignore my core,
To rid myself.

But this doesn't help,
Doesn't heal,
Mend,
Fix.

Me.

The toll,
The end result,
On my inner being,
Is *this*.

This hyper-visible mass,
This weight,
This pressure,
This space.

A consequence of Trauma,
And my wicked karma,
My only reward,
In the end.

Little Black Dress

This beautiful mess,
In this little black dress,
Fights me,
Until I admit to its request.

I can't fit it,
Can't mold it,
Can't shape it,
Into the ways my body flows.

A piece sticking here,
A piecing sticking there,
A sight I can't bear,
And an embarrassment I can't share.

This reflection baffles me,
Startles me,
Taunts me,
And won't leave me to my grief.

I hold my breath,
To suck in my body,
To conceal this ugliness,
that I wholeheartedly embody.

This mass,
The aches,
The pains,
Haunts me.

I leap,
I screech,
I weep,
Defeat.

The thoughts come to mind,
Which forces me to acknowledge intrusive thoughts,
That this cloth can't hide me,
And show me my hidden exquisite delicacy.

This horrid mess,
Trapped inside this little black dress,
Entwined between the smothering satin,
That's causing me grave distress.

Feelings of beauty escape me,
Reminders of failed attempts bully me,
To remind me of the pressure around my thighs,
And the mass surrounding my body.

The dress continues to shrink,
Snap goes the threading,
And the dress tears,
Which is the moment I've been dreading.

I couldn't fit it,
Couldn't mold it,
Couldn't shape it,
Into the ways my body flows.

Fat sticking here,
Fat sticking there,
A sight I must bear,
In a life that's not fair.

Shimmering Skies

Shimmers, Shimmers,
Above my eyes,
Your heavenly light,
Darkness' sole prize.

Glistening dots,
Dazzling majesty,
Part of reality,
Or my fantasy.

Dim, dimmed,
From my nightly gaze,
Gone now,
From the eyes you amaze.

Your identity,
Serenity,
Luminescent,
Incandescent.

Here among,
Us common folk,
Fear of our intrusion,
on the beauty that you invoke.

Incomparable,
To your presence,
Though we intimidate,
Your essence.

Still your perfection,
Shimmers on,
Without disruption,
Or damage done.

Earth's rays,
Upon your eyes,
Dim your glow,
And diminish my pride.

Your light,
Fought my darkness,
Your sparkles,
Lifted my carcass.

But you must retreat,
Behind your blinds,
As I am left down here,
For a purpose I must find.

Until you return,
I bid farewell,
For your beauty,
I must bid well.

Split

There's this tree that I remember from my childhood,
A tree that was split in two,
And still remained standing.

I would often frolic between the gapping space,
Attempt to repair the damage,
Thinking that I could bandage its wound.

The tree sat there,
Continued to attend to its needs,
And the needs of the life that inhabits it.

Broken, but whole,
Has become a daily mantra,
For my heart's cry for help.

Anatomically whole, but metaphorically broken,
To live, to breathe, to exist,
In a world of such perfection.

How to mend the gapping space inside of my body,
To breathe without assistance of my body's cry for help,
In a desperate attempt to escape my mind's insanity.

Maybe if I was split like that imperfect tree,
Carved from the soil of god's hands.

I could breathe freely again,
Without fear of myself,
As a broken, but whole being.

A being not capable of much,
A space not asking for anything,
Towards a momentarily slither of hope.

Him

There's a beauty in his smile,
His captivating stance,
That makes me uneasy,
and makes my heart do a dance.

Performing for you,
Relinquishing my body,
Letting go of all morals,
Just to ensure that our worlds are shared.

My apologies for maintaining my composure,
My strength,
My neutrality,
My obscurity.

My fantasies of your voice among mine,
Warms me,
Assures me,
That pain isn't all that this life holds for me.

Even though our worlds are far apart,
I still want to thank you,
For showing me that my face can form a smile,
That my heart can sing another song,
That my emotions can experience joy.

I keep running away,
Trying to reassure myself,
That I have to go now,
That I can't do this,
That this can't be,
This feeling can't exist.

But the beauty of your smile,
Your captivating aroma,
Gives me vertigo,
Unlike the seasons.

I try to stay strong,
To not go against my own teachings,
My own guidance,
And my own struggles.

If I go through with this,
My insufficiencies will be gravely visible,
And you will see them,
And use them against me.

I try not to think these things,
Try not to imagine a world as your mule,
As your footstool,
But the way your smile awakens me is something I've
never experienced,
Heard of,
Nor dreamt of.

I have to go,
Not to resist the temptation of you,
But to repair myself for me.

I'll still think of you,
Sometimes, often, daily,
And remember the way you smiled at me,
Those few words that confirmed my existence.

I must focus on me,
Build me,
Heal me,
Because I only got me.

Someday, there will be a beauty in my smile,
My captivating stance,
That makes people uneasy,
And makes their heart do a dance.

I just gotta get there,
Before you find me.

Birthday Blues

Birthday blues,
Blues of age,
Blues of failure,
Blue emotions.

What a lovely time of year,
When the clock strikes twelve,
And when my escape from the womb,
Should be of upmost importance.

A dreadful tune,
Plays on loop,
A tune that reminds me of my failures,
All on a day that is supposed to be mine.

Why must my heart break so,
Shatter on the ground,
And why must I trample on the broken pieces,
And weep at their destruction.

I wish I was enjoying this day,
Relishing each moment,
Wishing for joy's consistency,
Instead of living off of past mistakes.

I must stop now,
Breathe lightly,
And prove to myself,
That I won't repeat years prior.

With my head down,
Hiding my shame,
My fears,
And my sorrow…

A familiar face,
Catches my attention,
A face I had fallen so hard for,
And made my heart smile.

I saw Him,
On a day that is mine,
In a moment that was his,
At a time that I needed.

Why must I attach my trauma to him,
Make Him to be the bad guy,
To cover up for myself,
And rebuke my affection for him.

I must admit that his face enlightened my day,
And affirmed my visibility,
But taught me,
The nuance of it all.

One minute,
I want Him,
The next minute,
I want just Me.

Both are impossible on this loop,
That goes on in my head,
This loop that keeps spinning and spinning,
And captures me beneath its feet.

I can't have it all,
Not on my birthday,
Not on any day,
Not one day.

Tomorrow, I will shed today,
To hide my demons from Him,
I will recover from this,
To resume my own Normal.

These Birthday blues,
Sound so melodic, but oh so real,
These Blues of age,
Relay my inner rage.

Blues of failure,
Blue emotions,
Blue not because of Him,
Blues because of birth.

B

B as in bitch,
A label that scarred me,
A term that birthed me,
The essence of what I still am.

B as in below, beneath,
A term that I've always been,
A truth that I've come accustomed to disguising,
From the people who would reveal my identity.

B as in big,
Big girl, big boobed girl, the boob,
The existence of this mass,
The volume of my body,
Hurt them so,
Cut them so,
As I slowly internalized each word,
And learned to resent this…. THING.

B as in "bigidity",
Though its real spelling is rigidity,
A nonexistent attitude brought on by my own insanity,
A flesh-eating infection that glued itself to me,
And ripped apart the very fabric of my words' true intent.

B as in beneath,
Beneath the ones that persecute me,
Beneath the ones that raise me up,
Beneath the ground that thirsts for my soul.

B,
Is that all that I will ever be,
Is that all that I have to look forward to,
All that I am capable of.

B,
As in this low score,
That taints my perfectionist record,
And reminds me of everything I lack.

I must try to break the chains of my oppressor,
Conquer the demons of my own mind,
Wipe away my tears,
And push old things aside.

Come forth,
B free,
Escape this wretched place,
I whisper to her.

I can't lift the stone,
Can't pull the sword,
Can't escape the cycle,
Of being trapped in my mind.

B bright, B present, B you,
She says.

All I can hear,
Are these dreadful words that slither from my memories,
Saying that B as in bitch,
B as in big,
B meaning average, beneath, catastrophe...

An identity that still courses through my veins,
Like slow-healing scars,
And slow drying tears.

B as in bitch,
A label that scarred me,
A term that birthed me,
The essence of what I will continue to fight against.

The big unveiling

My face I can't show,
The emotions I must hide,
The plight I must endure,
With no one to confide.

The features I can't fake,
These emotions I can't break,
The answers I must face,
The commitment that I must embark.

To hide from me,
To conceal me,
To project you,
Back onto me.

The world is full of blissful beings,
Beings who reflect smiles,
Possess positivity,
And uphold normality.

This creation I've construed,
Mimics the faces that I see,
To hide the emotions I can't confront,
To protect me from the girl I can't free.

Your projection becomes my possession,
With my soul draining your life forces,
Fixing my inner spirit,
To avoid a public meltdown.

These emotional wounds healed by wet band-aids,
Should not be able to escape my lips,
Or disclose my apathy,
Towards my own functional inabilities.

There's a mask that I put on,
A mask that I've already held on to,
A mask built upon your happiness,
To prevent a fuss from being made over me.

This mask protected me from me,
To blend in with theses drones,
Protected you from me,
And these troubled emotions I withhold.

Must I hide so,
And hide my message,
These visual,
And my emotional cues.

I must,
To conform,
To blend in,
To not cause a fuss.

I won't show my face,
I will hide my emotions,
Because this path that I must endure,
Takes no prisoners.

Good Enough

Am I,
Even enough,
Enough to fit,
Enough to exist.

Am I,
Worthy enough,
Enough to be,
Enough to breathe.

Will they,
Decipher me,
Decode me,
And strip my outer being.

Do I,
Confess to,
My disguise,
And my fragmented lies.

My mediocrity,
My failed attempts,
To imitate, comply,
For my victor's indulgence.

How can they,
Rip apart,
Decry,
My fragmented creation.

How can I,
Let them,
Control,
My story.

How can I,
Surrender to,
The obvious victors,
My valiant contenders.

I gave,
      All
            Of
                 ME.

To present,
My essence,
To validate,
My presence.

Only to concede,
To my fate,
As second rate,
Against my victor's stakes.

But I,
Exemplified my,
Exquisite art,
My master craft.

Good enough,
To fit,
Good enough,
To exist.

Worthy enough,
To breathe,
In spite of,
What they believe.

Tightrope

grasping the balancing pole,
in my hand,
i assume my position,
on the stand.

one foot forward,
the other behind,
i take a deep breath,
and straighten my spine.

onward, onward,
across the tightrope,
i grip my bearings,
and hold on to hope.

envisioning my weight,
shifting the rope,
my breaths deepen,
as I try to cope.

one hand falters,
as it disengages from the pole,
the other steadies,
to do as it was told.

the hand tugs,
and gnaws at the other,
as if failure has become,
my one and only lover.

balance, I cannot,
as evidenced by my hopeless face,
as failure has driven me,
into a cold, dark place.

i didn't scream,
didn't make a fuss,
because I've become accustomed to,
life treating me like dust.

but they can't see,
me up high,
nor hear my screech,
or my silent cry.

i fell,
all the way down,
from my tightrope,
elevated above the ground.

no one to assist,
not a sound to be made,
as my monstrous screech,
began to fade.

they surrounded me,
and looked at me in shame,
began spitting on the ground,
because I was the one to blame.

stuck in midair,
with my torn disguise,
falling into their pool of spit,
in my bed of lies.

wasn't
        good
                enough,
nowhere to hide,
nowhere to retreat,
no one to confide.

falling falling FALLING,
down down DOWN,
in their spit,
upon the ground.

they surrounded me,
and looked at me in shame,
I fell in their pool of spit,
and I was the one to blame.

Visible

I sat there,
Starved for attention,
But dreading the outcome.

I wanted to be seen,
But not to be on focus,
And not overlooked.

I want to be seen,
Sitting there on the borders of shame,
And hiding my head in my hands.

Hoping someone's eyes will see me,
Rather overlook me,
To call upon my birth name.

A call echoes from their lips,
And I am on display,
To both my dismay and content.

I am summoned by a name that isn't my own.
Which makes me force a smile,
To be content that I wasn't overlooked.

I wanted to be seen,
But not to be called upon,
By a name that I don't own.

Once again, I am in the spotlight,
As this name continues to be called,
And pestered for a response.

I accept the calling,
Ignore my heart begging me to speak up,
And giving in to my mind's wishes of shutting up.

I wanted to be made visible,
To be made wanted,
To be made.

My lips trapped behind my mind's zipper,
Tries to force out a plea,
A plea to correct.

This anomaly among these masses,
Admitting to their mistake,
Becomes my shortcomings.

Becoming a symptom of me,
Seems to be the status quo,
Among these folks.

Forgetfulness and mindless responses,
Shape their perceptions,
And harnesses their vision.

Did you see me,
Hear me,
Or even smell me.

Did you see my figure,
Hear my pleas,
Or smelled my stench.

I wanted to be acknowledged,
To be vividly seen,
And to be respected.

I wanted to be called upon by my birth name,
The name that was chosen for me,
Rather than something your ill-advised memory
manufactured.

I can't let this damage my already broken spirit,
Destroy my will to live up to MY Name,
In a failed attempt to appease your ego.

Because I remember that I just sat there,
Not making a sound,
And not asserting my presence.

You reminded me of that,
Of the power that I could have,
And the power that I should project.

You saw me,
Saw my vulnerability,
Saw my disemboweled soul.

No more,
Not again,
And not soon.

See me,
Hear me,
Smell my presence.

I Matter,
Because I am Here,
And I am ready to be made Visible.

fairy god mother

The Summer I lost Myself

Strength, resilience, confidence,
Terms that should have kept me safe,
That could have held me,
That once told me everything would be alright.

They failed,
I failed,
Failure that screams out from my heart,
That echoes in the back of my mind,
Making me feel insufficient.

Insufficient, weak, incompetent,
Terms that convey my feelings,
Feelings that present this heavy pillow,
That's smothering me so.

Why can't this feeling be shaken?
This one bad mark,
This deep scar,
This harsh thought,
That I somehow let her down.

Who you may ask?

It's that girl who was confused,
That girl who was ridiculed for wasting her life,
A life she didn't ask for,
A life that she wishes would have ended years prior.

That girl who faced shame from her mother,
A woman that's supposed to offer support,
Supposed to be caring,
Supposed to be understanding,
Supposed to be encouraging.

The constant screams of taking unnecessary breaks,
After graduation,
The continuous name calling,
Endured over her life.

I feel like I can't breathe,
Can't see,
Can't think.

I've made it this far,
Spent countless restless nights studying,
Constant self-care days to rest,
Only to end it with this gut-wrenching feeling of being
average.

This summer has been hard, stressful...
Excuses aren't valid here,
Never here,
Nor the place I used to call home.

How many pills does it take,
How many slits does it take,
How many ropes does it take,
To end it, to finish it,
To destroy the anomaly among this species.

The summer when I lost it all,
In that empty parking lot,
With that life-threatening message,
Among the chatter of life's other inhabitants.

"I don't think that I can give you an A"…
An award I never asked for,
A score that I never demanded,
An accomplishment that shouldn't be given.

I struggle now,
I must go,
I can't go on,
Finishing this,
Living this,
Covering for this lie.

I'm living another life,
A life not my own,
A persona that must I escape,
Escape from this pit of despair.

I can feel her nails,
Scraping against my outer core,
She can't be within this ugly being,
Her freedom is of her upmost importance.

She reminds me of that summer when I lost it all,
In a parking lot that wasn't empty,
In a life with piercing eyes ridiculing me.

She must go,
I must go,
To that other side,
The safer side,
Of all of the trashed anomalies,
Before I let her go.

Hear

I can hear her cries,
Feel her breath,
Tears streaming down my chest.

The whimpers, the pain, the anguish,
Muffle my voice,
And paralyze my movements.

It's lonely up here,
Down here,
EVERYWHERE.

She can't breathe,
Her heart beats to her own song,
A never-ending tune.

Hark, goes her voice!
No one turns,
No one moves.

Silence.

There are voices now,
Voices of pity,
Voices of shame,
Voices of hate.

Her cries grow louder,
With each passing moment,
Moments that increase her anguish.

No one's listening,
No one cares,
NOONE is THERE.

The cries grow louder,
And louder,
And LOUDER!

Breath, tears,
Flashbacks to the past,
Play on loop in her mind.

She moves her mouth to scream,
But she stops,
Fearing retaliation, hatred, ridicule.

Her cries suddenly stop,
The tears cease,
Heartbeat steadies.

I hand her a tissue,
The same tissue that's always been here,
That's always been there.

She stands up now,
And looks at me,
With those dark, gloomy eyes.

I hold her hand,
She wraps her arm around mines,
As her hair blows through the wind.

One breath, one step, one leap,
Gravity pushes her down,
Steady as she goes.

Over, over, OVER,
Red has always been a beautiful color,
In the summertime.

Lavender

Sitting here,
In this dingy stained waiting area,
Waiting, hoping, but dreading of being called.

Dreading to hear my name,
Summoned back,
Into the lavender stained office.

Soothing lavender,
Calming lavender,
The scent that leaves me unguarded.

Time goes on,
Minutes plague me,
Before I am finally called.

I follow her fair skin,
Down a never-ending hallway,
To her office of neutral-colored walls.

As I take my seat on the dingy, colored couch,
The rink of lavender seeps into the room,
And starts to make all pains drift away.

My life,
Outlined through each vapor,
Strung up to unveil my truth.

I can see the vapor seep through her hair strands,
Revealing my weaknesses,
And leaving me unguarded.

She uses my mind against me,
Unravel my insecurities,
And banishing my faults.

Is this what is allowed to happen,
To submit to a specialist,
To align my thoughts to seemingly *act* normal.

I've faced the music,
Stood before her,
To show her my growing pains.

I don't want to be here,
Why does she want me to be here,
and why am I *Here*.

She can't help me,
A thought pattern often protested,
While tempting me with lavender.

I confirm that I am not a textbook case,
As my trials are present,
And have given themselves faces.

This talking shit won't work for me,
As my voice has grown weak,
Due to a shell of my own design.

The smell of damp air enters the room,
And I reflect on what brought me here,
And what made me seek this help.

I thought I was strong,
I thought that I was supposed to handle *it*,
Supposed to forget about *it*.

Why do these troublesome memories haunt me,
Keep pestering me,
Keep being replayed in my mind.

I go now,
Retreat to my shell,
To escape the calmness of this lavender.

I must go back,
To my happy place,
In an attempt to hold it together.

Because if I crack,
Just for one second,
In this very moment…

They'll catch up to me,
She'll catch on to me,
And find me slipping.

The tears I can't shed,
The pain I can't face,
And the scars that I can't heal.

Sweet lavender,
Calming lavender,
Leave me be.

Fucking Therapy

I'm so fucking tired,
Tired of the false hopes,
False dreams,
And ridiculous puns.

No, I'm not fucking alright,
I'm so tired,
Tired of my energy being drained,
Tired of being told that this is my responsibility,
And tired of being HERE.

Yea, I know, I know,
This shit they call therapy is supposed to work,
Supposed to calm those inner demons,
And help me find my strength.

Ha, this shit is a gimmick,
A waste of my fucking time,
A time I could have spent constructively,
Cutting, pill popping, drinking, and eating,
Until death do us part.

The Lord hasn't been terribly kind,
Making me wait so long for death,
Why am I still here,
When life has thrown me around like this for so long.

I've been chewed,
Gnawed,
Stepped on,
All in the name of "therapy."

Why am I not healed yet,
Not relishing in my life,
Not content with days' obscurity,
And open to try new things.

Stop fucking looking at me,
I have nothing to say,
Nothing to live for,
And nothing to wish for.

Goals they say,
Goals that I can't reach,
Goals I cannot envision,
Goals that aren't feasible.

Can't you fucking see I'm stuck in the trenches,
My brain won't allow me to get up,
My legs fail me,
And ridicule all these ridiculous pains.

So don't ask me again,
Am I alright?
No, I'm not,
And never will be.

But you know what,
That's ok.

I've felt like this for over 20 years,
Been at this point for as long as I can remember,
Thought like this before I knew words' meaning,
And envisioned my future like this.

There's no changing,
No fixing this,
No repairing broken bonds,
No picturing a life without these thoughts.

I'm shutting down now,
Like I should have been doing,
So no restarting my body,
And no backing up my thoughts.

Am I alright,
You deliberately ask again,
With your worried face,
I force my mouth, my heart, and my spirit,
To say that I am indeed alright.

Drugged

I can't fathom their feelings,
Their worry,
Their fear,
Of me taking my own life.

Drugged up,
Keeps me in suspense,
Traps me in time,
And chains me to my own sorrow.

Why can't they let me go,
On that other side of the road,
The side of darkness,
To my ending.

Doped up,
Calm now,
Is what they want,
To ease their own conscience.

Tied up,
Restrained to my room,
Kept to myself,
To regain control.

Breathe girl,
You've felt this before,
Ignore it,
Deflect it.

Pains seeping through,
The ecstasy they put me through,
Spinning,
Losing control.

I must fight,
To get her back,
The her that wants to leave,
The her that yearns for my ending.

Why is she weakening,
The part of my soul that has my strength,
The part that has the answers,
The part that enlightens my walk.

Enemies,
Is what they are,
To remedy my heartache,
To appease their interests.

Release me,
From these drugs,
This prison,
This calmness.

On my way up,
Clawing my way through the cracks,
Releasing myself,
Breathing heavily.

Flushing down the calmness,
Filtering out the shame,
Of what I should be like,
Of who I am.

Transparent

It's like you can see right through me,
Through my paper skin,
Through my painful grin.

It's like my pain is plastered on my face,
Strung up like barrettes through my hair,
To make all who see aware.

The faces you give to my inner demons,
The reasoning that you place in my mind,
To help me escape my bind.

Why must you reveal my scars,
To those who ridicule my emotions,
And who set my insanity in motion.

My skin flaking below your feet,
Revealing pains that haven't manifested,
And inviting emotions that I've divested.

Fleeing from your presence,
To escape your mirror of truth,
To keep my ocean from escaping too.

I'm stranded from my lifeline,
That part of me that hid this,
That part of me that I miss.

Knowing I need you,
Not wanting you,
To delve deeper into,
My roots.

You saw me,
And then you saw her,
And killed her.

It's like you saw right through me,
At her paper skin,
Through my painful grin.

How can you fathom a silent scream,
Dissect each tear,
And banish all fear.

It's like I can see you,
Watching you unravel,
Each of my battles.

Through you,
I can see my getaway,
Once used as her entryway.

My oceans play like trumpets,
To my own ballad,
A tune that assures that my pain is valid.

You came,
You saw,
You released her,
Afar.

It's Me

It's not you,
It's me,
Your feeble attempts,
Although noble,
Aren't working.

It's me,
Not you,
With my flawed thoughts,
Although true,
Are a hindrance.

Me with my ways,
With my instability,
Though abrupt,
As my nemesis.

It's not you,
It's me.

Let's part here,
Let's cease here,
Let us end this,
Although enchanting,
But dreadful.

It's me,
Not you,
Your failed attempts to not make this a chore,
Although appreciative,
But lies.

What you taught me,
What I have taught you,
Reflects in my words,
Every scribble,
Every stroke.

It's you,
Not me,
With your one-sided answers,
Although truthful,
Not necessary.

It's you,
With your by the book explanation,
Of what I am,
Although broken,
Not shattered.

It's us,
That's responsible,
For this tragedy of existence,
Although your fault,
But my quest.

It's me.

Fix Me

Heal me,
fix me,
turn me,
into,
a work of art.

Shape me,
build me,
mold me,
erase,
my life's curse.

Soothe me,
comfort me,
embrace me,
undo,
this pain.

Loosen the,
threads that,
restrict me,
from,
Perfect alignment.

The chemicals,
Abuse me,
Scar me,
Inside,
My brain.

That's it,
Right there,
Chemically align,
Them,
Make me free.

      Sew.
          Me.
               Back.
                  Up.

glass slipper

These Stars

These stars,
Your stars,
Our stars.
Staring directly into our souls.

They're beautiful,
You're beautiful,
We're beautiful,
Unlike this life that was chosen.

Twinkling there,
Twinkling here,
Twinkling everywhere,
Stars.

Heard talk of these dippers,
These patterns,
Your patterns,
Our patterns.

They're making room for this pain,
Your pain,
Our pain,
Concealing, shadowing, protecting.

These stars,
Your stars,
Our stars,
Are up there.

Watching, lingering, searching,
For the end,
Your end,
Our end.

How much does it cost to be a dipper,
To write myself within those patterns,
To allow myself to be seen, gazed upon, on display.

Them stars,
So beautiful, so peaceful, so heavenly,
The way they concealed, shadowed, protected them
dippers.

Wallowing at the tail end of that dipper,
There is a faint touch,
A weak caress,
A tired hand.

To touch the helm of these dippers,
your dippers,
our dippers.

To feel that beauty,
That veil,
Your veil,
Our veil.

I'll gladly pay the toll,
To be a part of that world,
Your world,
The world.

Among those dippers,
Those patterns,
Those stars,
Emerges a faint beam.

It fades quickly,
The moment passes,
The veil soars,
The feeling subsides.

How wonderful would it have been,
To be a part of that place,
Among those stars,
Belonging, existing, remaining.

These stars,
Your dippers,
The world,
Remains unshaken.

Validation

Validation speaks,
Amongst the remnants of life,
Calms my weeping heart.

Another Round

Take my hand into yours,
She whispers softly to me,
Let's escape our demons,
And find our free.

One slit,
Is all it would take,
To lose consciousness,
And take the pain away.

My silent screech,
Never caused a stir,
So I crept into the bathroom,
And my demons concur.

Spreading my body,
Across the dirty vinyl floor,
Drained from last week's mess,
In my clothes from the night before.

Press as hard as you can,
With the tip of your knife,
Let those juices pour,
To end your life.

Your life yields no value,
My demons decree,
So surrender now,
She whispers to me.

My voiceless screech,
That they can't hear,
The continuous pain,
That shackles me here.

They stole my vision,
Erased my dream,
And left me with scars,
From their wicked scheme.

Inside my empty shell,
Of loneliness and pity,
Makes me seem,
Ever so bitty.

Painful wet eyes,
Cloud my vision,
She took the blade,
To finish our mission.

One slit,
Is all it would take,
To lose consciousness,
And take the pain away.

As my demons rejoice,
To acknowledge my end,
Makes me consider,
My plan once again.

Looking down,
At the pierced blade,
Enables me to reflect,
On the plans I've made.

Staring into the wet eyes,
Of the face of my pain,
Makes me remember,
The life they've slain.

They clouded my vision,
Tarnished my dream,
And left me with scars,
From their wicked scheme.

Standing tall,
Without my frown,
I part my lips,
To request another round.

Ignite

I wanna be ignited,
And to be heard,
For people to stare,
At my every word.

I want this fire on my tongue,
To set my heart on fire,
To teach me not to reflect,
On years prior.

Look up at me,
From beneath your feet,
Listen to my words,
And hear me weep.

Toss a coin,
In my overflowing well,
Wish for my fire,
To make me well.

The oceans that I cried,
Have dimmed my light,
Help start me up,
Make me ignite.

Focus your mind,
Ignore me no longer,
Cause it is time,
For me to be stronger.

I wanna be ignited,
By your wicked grace,
I wanna be seen,
As part of this place.

My reflection forms,
Against the mirror of time,
My conscience grows clear,
Of your crime.

Toss your coin,
To claim your luck,
But I'll be here,
On your way up.

Ignite me,
With your words of spite,
Beat against me,
With all your mite.

Focus your heart,
On the pain I've felt,
It's time for you,
To play the hand I've been dealt.

Slowly and slowly,
You'll plan your retreat,
Because my angels will surely see,
To your defeat.

Watch my dance,
As I ignite,
And I'll watch you,
Take your own life.

The pains,
That you put me through,
Are all reflected,
Back at you.

My ignition,
Resumes its normal pace,
I'm visible,
And a part of this space.

You didn't ignite me,
But that's OK,
I've finally learned how,
To keep you demons at bay.

thanks for listening.

-excerpt from a letter I wrote my therapist

you have
my
blood
on
your hands
how
glorious
it is
to trade
our pains
to
create
something
as beautiful
as this

Made in the USA
Coppell, TX
18 December 2021